CUBA

TRAVEL GUIDE

*Explore Culture, Cuisine, and
History in Havana and Beyond*

By Tamara Marie

Contents

Introduction to Cuba

Cuba is a Caribbean island only 90 miles off the coast of Florida. It is one of the nearest neighbors to the United States, yet one of the hardest for US citizens to visit. The country is an exciting blend of African and Caribbean culture, from the vibrant art and music scene to the relaxed beaches, vineyards, tobacco fields, and sugar plantations. It is the largest of the Caribbean islands and home to 11 million people of various ethnic tribes, expats, and more.

Cuba is divided into 15 administrative regions, but for the purposes of this book we'll be referring to Eastern, Central, and Western Cuba as the main regions. These each have 5 provinces within them and are vastly different from one another.

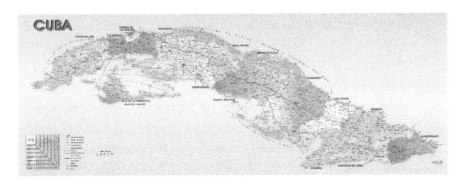

Eastern Cuba is home to some of the island's largest mountains, most beautiful beaches, and oldest cities. Cuba's first capital, Santiago, lies in the eastern region and it has a very different character than its western counterpart, Havana.

Western Cuba is the farmland of the country. This is where to find the tobacco fields and coffee plantations, nestled among the brightly colored bougainvillea and quiet beaches. Stark mogotes contrast the rolling green mountains on the east. These sharp limestone plateaus hide a network of caves, including the one that housed Che Guevara during the Cuban missile crisis. Havana lies in the north of the region, along a natural harbor, and is without a doubt one of the most cosmopolitan cities in the country.

Central Cuba is split in half by the main highway, the Carretera Central, which links Havana to Santiago. The southern half of Central Cuba is made up of the Sierra del Escambray mountain range, known for lush rainforests, striking waterfalls, and sugar plantations. The northern half of the region is flatter and more agricultural, home to dairy and pineapple farms, among others.

The main tourist cities in Cuba are Havana, Baracoa, Trinidad, Cienfuego, Santiago, Santa Clara, Pinar del Rio, and Varadero. Not all of these are among the largest cities in Cuba. Some of Cuba's largest cities are more industrial and often skipped by travelers in favor of historical or natural attractions.

The capital of Cuba is Havana, but it wasn't always that way. Santiago, in the far east, was the first capital until it was decided that Havana had a better harbor. There is a fierce rivalry between the two cities; Santiago often considers itself more "Cuban" than Havana, which was heavily influenced by the Spanish and the Americans.

Havana is the international airport, however, and this is where you'll fly into. Plan at least two or three days to let Havana embrace you before heading into the more remote regions of Cuba.

Havana is bold and brash, a city five times larger than any other city in Cuba, and full of juxtaposition. Grand neoclassical mansions among slums, an extravagant malecon with junk fishing boats on the shore, an old city inside now non-existent walls, a new and vibrant city that continues to grow.

Chapter One: Cuban History

Cuba's history began thousands of years ago, when it was inhabited by three indigenous Amerindian tribes, the Taino, Guanajatabey, and the Ciboney. These tribes came from across the South American continent and other Caribbean islands. Even today the cultures are very interlinked.

The arrival of the Spanish changed the landscape of Cuba. Christopher Columbus made landfall on October 28, 1492. The first settlement was at Baracoa and the second was at what is now Havana. Cuba remained a Spanish colony until 1898, when the Spanish-American War took place.

Early History

Cuba has staged several revolutions over the span of its life. The first occurred in 1868, when a plantation owner called for a revolution and freed his slaves so that they could fight alongside him. Thousands of indentured servants died during the Ten Years War, which ended in 1878 when Spain granted Cuba more autonomy, but not full independence.

In the early 1890s, exiled Cuban Jose Marti created the Cuban Revolutionary Party while living in New York. He returned to Cuba to garner support for his cause in 1895 and was subsequently killed at the Battle of Dos Rios less than a month later.

Jose Marti

His cause was championed and there were thousands of Cuban guerilla fighters, although not enough to beat the Spanish. In order to "protect" Cuban civilians, the military governor general, Spanish-born Valeriano Weyler, herded them into camps. We would now term these concentration camps. Nearly 400,000 Cubans died of starvation in the camps.

Within weeks, Europeans and Americans protested the Spanish treatment of Cubans. The US sent the Maine, which was blown up in Havana Harbor. While unclear as who did it, the Spanish were of course blamed.

This was the beginning of the short-lived Spanish-American War.

The war ended with the Treaty of Paris in December 1898. Spain relinquished much of their remaining empire, including Cuba, the Philippines, Guam, and Puerto Rico. The United States took control of all of these, allowing Cuba to be essentially independent but under US control.

Independent Cuba as a US Protectorate

Full Cuban independence took effect in 1902, but under the Platt Amendment the United States retained one foot in the proverbial door. These seven points are listed in the Cuban Constitution, and boil down to the fact that the United States did not want to relinquish full control of Cuba but wanted the world to see them as a benevolent power. Cuba might have been independent, but the US still controlled much of their political power. The Platt Amendment also stipulated that the US be able to lease military land, leading to the still-ongoing control of Guantanamo Bay naval base.

Fulgencio Batista

Cuba had several presidents over the following forty years. The most well known of these was the last, Fulgencio Batista, the leader of the Sergeants Revolt in 1933. He was elected president in 1934, and is thus far the only non-white to win a Cuban presidential election.

He lost the following two elections and then staged a coup, taking down Carlos Prio Socarras in 1952. Batista remained president until forced into exile in 1958 when the Castro brothers and Che Guevara masterminded a revolution.

Revolution

In the early 1950s, Fidel Castro and close to a hundred supporters fought their way from Santiago, in the southeast, to Havana in the northwest. They were inadvertently helped by US President Eisenhower, who imposed the arms embargo to stifle the rebels, but ended up hurting Batista's government military more.

Che Guevara and Fidel Castro

By 1959, Batista had fled to Dominica and later to Portugal, where he finally settled. The Castro brothers and Che began to impose their own rule on the country. They put Manuel Urrutia Lleo in the presidential seat, although Fidel Castro was undoubtedly the real leader, and they executed hundreds of Batista followers.

For another six years, there were uprisings against the new regime, but Castro's followers quelled each insurgency.

Dwight Eisenhower

Rather than respond to Castro's request for arms, Eisenhower kept the arms embargo in place. Castro began purchasing military supplies from the Soviet Union. Additionally, as US companies in Cuba refused to do Castro's bidding, he nationalized them.

Political Tensions

In the early 1960s, Eisenhower began planning to overthrow the Castros, in what is known as the Bay of Pigs invasion. He also imposed a stricter trade embargo on Cuban products in 1960. The invasion took place during President John F. Kennedy's term, on

April 14, 1961. The nearly 1,500 CIA-trained Cuban exiles didn't manage to overthrow the Castros, however. Whether in direct result to the failed invasion or because the US refused to supply arms to Cuba, Cuba signed a secret deal with the Soviets to place nuclear missiles on the island.

The situation finally deescalated in 1962 when the Soviets publicly agreed to remove their missile launchers from Cuba and the US secretly agreed to remove their Jupiter ballistic missiles from Turkey. Cuba stayed close to the Soviets. Relations continued to sour, however, and in February 1962, President Kennedy imposed travel restrictions from the US to Cuba which lasted until 2014, when President Obama relaxed the arms embargo and reopened the US embassy in Havana.

What do the Travel Restrictions Mean?

The travel restrictions as imposed by President Kennedy are no longer in effect. Times are vastly different than they were back then and it is easier to visit Cuba now more than ever before in many of our lives.

Today's restrictions mean that you must travel under a special general license category, which are outlined below, but many US carriers have opened direct flights to Cuba from New York, Miami,

Chicago, and Los Angeles. We will touch on more visa and licensing details in the next chapter.

Chapter Two: What to Know Before You Go

In this section we'll touch on the practical knowledge needed to travel to Cuba, things like "what language do they speak?", "what is the local currency?", and "what side of the road do they drive on?". We'll expand on this section in later chapters, so consider this the bullet points of what you need to know before you go.

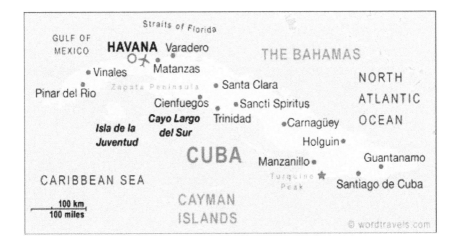

Language

Cubans speak Spanish, so knowing some of the language is definitely preferable. They do, however, speak a distinct dialect so while your high school Spanish may be passable, you may find it difficult to understand the locals. You can pick up a copy of **Cuban Spanish 101** before you go, so you'll be prepared and understand most of the unique Cuban words and expressions (paperback and E-book available on Amazon).

Time zone

Cuba is in the UTC -5 time zone, or the same as US Eastern Standard Time. They observe daylight saving time.

Currency

Cuba has two currencies. The first is the local currency, which is known as the *monada nacional*, or national money. It is the Cuban Peso, or CUP. Tourists will hardly ever use this currency, since hotels, restaurants, taxis, and more don't accept it. You could use it at street vendors or local Cuban cafes, where the clientele is all Cuban, but in all likelihood you will not have the need. The second currency is the CUC, or Cuban Convertible Peso. This is what you will use to pay for hotels, bars, meals, and more. It was created to be on par with the US dollar.

Moneda Nacional

It is also advisable to have enough cash on hand for your entire visit. ATMs are few and far between, and American debit and credit cards will not work in the country. Some sources say that they will, but recent travelers have said that they don't (January 2017). If you have a foreign card, expect a high fee, sometimes near 3% even for a Visa card. Canadian dollars, Euros, and British Pound Sterling are all accepted forms of currency as well.

Power Outlets

Cuban power outlets are the same as the United States. You will not need an adaptor. The electrical voltage is generally 110V/60Hz but in newer hotels may be 220V/60Hz.

Internet and Phone Service

It is also worth noting that internet access and phone service is VERY scarce in Cuba. Most hotels do not have Wi-Fi or even internet cables, so you should have most of your major accommodation and cars booked in advance.

Driving in Cuba

Cubans drive on the right side of the road, like we do in the US. Renting a car in Cuba is expensive and if you're going less than 150km (93.2 miles) away, according to Lonely Planet, it is easier and cheaper to hire a taxi. Cuba, like almost every other country in the world, uses the metric system. Distances will be in kilometers and speed limits km/hour. To convert, you need to know that one km is equal to .62 miles. This means that 100km/h is approximately 62 mph. Most speed limits in Cuba are 100 km/hour.

 Your home license is enough to rent a car with, but make sure you have your passport with you when hiring the car. You will have to put down a deposit; if you have an accident and are at fault, you will not get your deposit back.

It is also advised to store the radio in the trunk of the car at night to avoid theft - it is the only thing you won't get covered for with the rental insurance!

Beware of Scams

Beware of local scams while in Cuba. This can be anything from offering to show you around, but taking much longer than they say and asking you to pay for the additional time to fake cigars and much more. It is well worth it to be on your guard.

Cuba is an exciting destination that many of us have been hoping to see for a long time. With the rules a little bit relaxed, there is the chance for Americans to visit legally. The next chapters will be in detail about the visa requirements needed for Cuba and how to travel there - legally!

Chapter Three: Traveling to Cuba

At only 90 miles off the US coast, Cuba was once a US protectorate and a popular tourist destination for many Americans. Since the Cold War, that relationship has soured and only recently thawed. The country has long been a popular destination for Canadians and Europeans, however, and the pictures of modern-day Cuba that we see still look like something out of an old movie. In this chapter, we'll cover the intangible "why should you go to Cuba?" along with the more practical visa and general licensing requirements and how to legally enter the country.

Why Should You Go to Cuba?

Cuba emits an almost mysterious quality. Because Americans still can't get into the country freely (i.e. on a visa waiver) and must be on one of the thirteen special licenses, many Americans haven't gone or are holding off on going until travel restrictions ease even further.

However, going before that happens means you'll still be able to catch a glimpse of old Cuba - the Communist era one, where the cars are still 1950s Chevys or Fords, where technology hasn't caught up with the rest of the world yet, and where life is a lively and energetic blend of cultures.

Some experts claim that - because Cuba has been exposed to western culture through the thousands of Europeans and Canadians that have been traveling there for decades - it won't be changed by American travel. It's likely that it will change, at least somewhat. As more and more Americans visit, more Cuban-Americans bring back money to families on the island, and technological advances are made greater, we will slowly change the face of Cuban culture.

There are tons of reasons to visit Cuba, like the fact that it still seems like forbidden fruit - that is often enough for a lot of people - or that the sooner you travel there, the less people you will encounter. Imagine traveling to Rome in high summer; Cuba will soon be like that!

Some of the intangible reasons to visit Cuba include the exotic culture, a melodious blend of West African and Caribbean, the enchanting, upbeat music, and the food.

Cuban Cigars

Of course, there are tangible reasons to visit Cuba, like the oak-aged rum, Havana cigars, and freshly roasted coffee. It is possible now to bring some of those home with you. Learn more at the end of this chapter.

Chapter Four: Introduction to Visas and General Licenses for Cuba

Thanks mainly to former US President Obama, the trade embargo that President Kennedy instituted was relaxed and travel restrictions were eased. Obama and Raul Castro first met - and publicly shook hands - at Nelson Mandela's South African funeral in December 2013. When Obama and his family visited in March 2016, it was touted as a new era in Cuban-American relations. Whether that will happen remains to be seen (as of 2017) but one thing is clear, Americans are excited to visit Cuba.

Raul Castro and US President Barack Obama

No longer do you have to route through Cancun or Nicaragua - two of the popular routing spots for travelers of before. Instead, all you need is a valid passport (be sure that the expiration date is at least six months after your trip ends), a visa, a general license that falls under one of thirteen categories, and an itinerary for your trip.

What is the difference between a visa and a general license?

The Cuban government requires all travelers to have a **visa**, regardless of where you come from. This is known as a "tourist card" and can be purchased at the check in counter of your airline. As time goes on, expect this to change but for now, it is $25-$100 USD (varies by airline!) and very easy to obtain. According to most sources, the visa process and cost is built into your ticket price if you purchase one in advance.

The Cuban tourist card is not the same as the **general license** that the US government requires. You still need to prove a schedule that does not include "tourist" activities, mainly for your own benefit, as it's possible you'll get questioned upon your arrival back into the US. It is worth noting that once you leave the US, no one will care or understand the general license, so if you have questions about it once you are in Cuba, you are best directing them to your travel agent or airline.

As mentioned above, there are thirteen categories for the general license. You do not need to apply for one through a government channel, but when filling out the OFAC (*Office of Foreign Assets Control*) card through your airline, you will have to state a reason that lines up with one of the thirteen.

Who decides what my general license category is?

You do. All you do is sign an affidavit when boarding the airline. Some airlines are including this in the online booking process, but it seems that most travelers are met at the gate by an agent who ensures you have both the US OFAC form and the Cuban tourist card. You are required, by the Department of Treasury, to keep receipts from your trip for five years, in case you need to prove that your trip to Cuba really was about humanitarian efforts.

Travel agents, journalists that have been to Cuba, airlines, and tour companies recommend keeping everything related to your Cuba trip in a file on your computer (a typed itinerary, airline receipts) and in a hard copy folder (general receipts from meals, hotels, any activities).

What are the thirteen general license categories?

The thirteen general license categories are:

1. family visits;
2. official business of the U.S. government, foreign governments, and certain intergovernmental organizations;
3. journalistic activity;
4. professional research and professional meetings;
5. educational activities;
6. people to people;
7. religious activities;
8. public performances, clinics, workshops, athletic and other competitions, and exhibitions;
9. support for the Cuban people;
10. humanitarian projects;
11. activities of private foundations or research or educational institutes;
12. exportation, importation, or transmission of information or informational materials;
13. and certain authorized export transactions.

The following definitions of each license are listed in the Department of Treasury special guides for Cuba PDF and the link is listed at the end of the chapter. For details regarding Cuba

travel, the US State Department is a good starting point:
https://travel.state.gov/content/passports/en/country/cuba.html

A **family visit license** can mean that you are traveling to visit your Cuban grandmother, whom you have never met, accompanying your mother to Cuba, or accompanying your half-sister to Cuba. *The Cuban government defines "close family" as "any individual related to a person "by blood, marriage, or adoption who is no more than three generations removed from that person or from a common ancestor with that person."*

An **official visit license** will be sanctioned by the US government, you will know if you qualify for this one!

A **journalistic activity license** covers "subject to conditions, full-time journalists, supporting broadcast or technical personnel, and freelance journalists to travel to Cuba. While it's hazy, since in the age of social media, we are all publishers and journalists, bloggers, take note: as long as you have a full work schedule, this also covers you.

The **professional research license** means that you can travel there to undertake "professional research in Cuba relating to a traveler's profession, professional background, or area of expertise." It has been expanded to include business meetings that fall under your professional area of expertise or "organization of such meetings by a traveler whose profession is related to the organization of professional meetings or conferences or who is an employee or contractor of an entity that is organizing the professional meeting or conference." Can you request international co-workers to meet you in Cuba for a business meeting? Yes, provided that you can prove that being in Cuba is beneficial to your business.

The **educational activities license** covers students and educators that are interested in study abroad programs. The category is quite broad and covers anyone wishing to engage in school programs or facilitate education among Cuban students. Students and educators are also authorized to participate in travel-related activities while in Cuba and the license covers a "reasonable" number of chaperones. Likewise, the **religious activities license** covers travelers wishing to pursue religious pursuits while in the country.

The **people-to-people license** covers travelers who wish to engage in meaningful people-to-people interactions with Cubans. This is by far the easiest license to categorize yourself under.

This means more than just chatting up the bartender or shopping (although by doing that you are both supporting the Cuban economy and interacting with the people).

The US government says: "Travelers utilizing this general license must ensure they maintain a full-time schedule of educational exchange activities intended to enhance contact with the Cuban people, support civil society in Cuba, or promote the Cuban people's independence from Cuban authorities, and that will result in meaningful interaction between the traveler and individuals in Cuba."

You will need an itinerary proving that you have met with organizations and people that facilitate people-to-people interactions.

Persons traveling to Cuba as part of a sports team or symphony group are subject to the **public performances, clinics, workshops, athletic and other competitions, and exhibitions license**. Like the educational and religious license, you are permitted to undertake "travel-related" activities while there.

Both support for the Cuban people and **humanitarian efforts** are recognized under the two licenses by each name. Support for the Cuban people is defined as participating in

"activities of recognized human rights organizations; independent organizations designed to promote a rapid, peaceful transition to democracy; and individuals and non-governmental organizations that promote independent activity intended to strengthen civil society in Cuba." Humanitarian projects can include medical or health projects, disaster preparedness, relief, or support, non-formal or formal education in any number of topics, environmental projects, or historical preservation. The full list, which is rather long, can be viewed at the OFAC link below.

OFAC's definition of the licensing for **activities of private foundations or research or educational institutes** is "travel-related transactions and other transactions that are directly incident to activities by private foundations or research or educational institutes with an established interest in international relations to collect information related to Cuba for noncommercial purposes, among other things." NGOs and nonprofits fall under this category, and OFAC has expanded the license to include persons that wish to establish an office for their organization on the island.

Under the **exportation, importation, or transmission of information or informational materials license**, travelers can deal in information, including music and artistic licensing. The expanded visa includes activities "directly incident to professional media or artistic productions of information or informational materials for exportation, importation, or transmission, including the filming or production of media programs (such as movies and television programs), the recording of music, and the creation of artworks in Cuba, provided that the traveler is regularly employed in or has demonstrated professional experience in a field relevant to such professional media or artistic productions." The final license category is for **certain authorized export transactions**, which is anything that doesn't fall under the above category.

What if my visit doesn't fall under one of the thirteen?

If your visit can't fall under one of the thirteen categories, you "aren't trying very hard," in the words of several travel bloggers. However, there are instances where it may not be possible to pigeonhole yourself into one of the thirteen categories, especially if you are not traveling for leisure reasons. For example, anyone wishing to do serious business in Cuba or any export transactions may not fall under the exportation category. In that case, you can apply for a special license under OFAC. This means that you DO need to apply directly to the US government for a license.

Applying for a special OFAC license:

https://www.treasury.gov/resource-center/sanctions/Pages/licensing.aspx

OFAC (Office of Foreign Assets Control) FAQs:
(https://www.treasury.gov/resource-center/sanctions/Programs/Documents/cuba_faqs_new.pdf)

There are always conditions associated with visas and licenses and these are no different. All of the thirteen licenses are subject to conditions, and all must have no more free time than a typical full-time schedule would allow.

If the US government thinks that your trip doesn't fall under the category that you signed for on the affidavit, you may be subject to lengthy questioning when you arrive back in the States. Based on various blogs, journalists, and new sources that have all visited Cuba within the last year, this is unlikely, but no one wants to rule it out. Additionally, with a new president in office, restrictions may be reinstated or travel fully revoked.

To ensure that your trip goes off without a hitch, you should keep a copy of your itinerary with you when traveling to and from the US, keep all travel transactions and records for five years (this is a requirement of the US government), and have a detailed list of your hotels and any contacts you have in Cuba.

Chapter Five: Costs Associated With the Visa and Licenses for Cuba

As stated above, costs for the Cuban tourist card appear to vary by airline. Technically, it is $50 USD, but some airlines are charging more and others are charging less. If you book in advance, it may only cost you $25-$50. It may also be included in the cost of your ticket, depending on your airline.

Again, this a vague point that sources disagree on. One thing is clear: the Cuban tourist card will cost you anywhere from $25 to $100 US dollars, and must be paid before you leave US soil. If you do not have one when you check in (i.e. you did not buy it online when you purchased your airline ticket), you will be directed to a separate desk to purchase one.

The Cuba tourist card/visa is valid for 180 days from the date of purchase and is only valid for a single-entry of no more than thirty days.

What else do I need to know about the visa and license?

Your Cuban tourist card/visa is a two part card. Both halves need to be filled out; they are identical. Upon arrival into Cuba, the customs and immigration officers will take one half. You need to keep the other one safe, as you will be required to submit it upon your departure.

Anyone traveling with minors needs to be aware that ALL travelers will need to fill out and sign an OFAC card, and have a Cuban tourist card. It would appear that this includes small children.

Am I ready to go to Cuba?

Once you have bought your visa and general license, you aren't quite ready to go.

Cuba requires that American travelers be covered under non-US insurance. As always, travel insurance is a very good idea, regardless of where you are going.

A good bet for this is World Nomads (Australia) travel insurance, but even they have some fine print regarding travel to Cuba. A Cuba-specific temporary insurance policy costs $25 USD, and is included in your airline ticket. In order to prove this, should you need to use the medical insurance while abroad, you need to keep your boarding pass while in the country.

Pre-Cuba Travel Checklist

Ensure you are ready for your trip with this handy checklist. We have divided it into two sections: time sensitive issues and everything else.

Time-sensitive issues:

▢ Arrange your travels. If you are joining a tour, make sure you have followed their deadlines for payment.

▢ If you are arranging your own flights, book at least six weeks in advance to get the best price. See the next chapter for details on airlines that fly to Cuba.

▢ Book a hotel. You may need to call to Cuba, as most accommodation does not have internet access. If you are traveling over a holiday, book well in advance to make sure you get the accommodation you prefer!

▢ Exchange money. This must be done before you leave the country as **US dollars cannot be exchanged in Cuba** without a 10% penalty. You also cannot get Cuban currency in the US. You will need to exchange your US dollars for Euros or British Pound Sterling and then exchange that again for Cuban currency once in Havana.

▢ Arrange travel insurance. Your flight cost includes medical insurance for Cuba, but travel insurance is always a good idea. You generally need to buy it before you go so that it covers your flights. World Nomads allows you to purchase it while you are on the road, however.

Everything else:

▢ Be sure your trip meets the US government regulations for civilian travel to Cuba (i.e. under one of the 13 general license categories). You will fill out an Office of Foreign Assets Control card at the airport before departing. You will not be allowed on the plane without one! It is not necessary to arrange it ahead of time (i.e. online).

⊠ Visa. Your Cuban tourist card, aka, your visa, is included in the cost of your airline ticket to Cuba. You will fill out the tourist card when you get to the airport for your flight.

⊠ Enjoy your trip!

Chapter Six: Airlines that Fly to Cuba

As travel restrictions eased, more and more American-based airlines started direct flights to Havana, Camaguey, Santa Clara, and Holguin. Unfortunately, some airlines have now started to discontinue service to Cuba. As of this writing, Southwest, Delta, American Airlines, JetBlue, Alaska, and Frontier all still have flights to Cuba, although they have cut back a bit on destinations. It's best to check with the individual airlines as to their current routes and scheduled flights.

Delta:
Delta Airlines flies daily, non-stop services to Havana from New York's JFK Airport, Miami International Airport, and Atlanta's Hartsfield Jackson International.

https://pro.delta.com/content/agency/sg/en/agent-resources/general-information/delta-scheduled-service-to-cuba--faqs-.html

JetBlue:

JetBlue was the first airlines to begin scheduled services to Cuba. Today, they offer flights to three different Cuban cities, where you can begin your adventure. From New York's JFK Airport and Orlando International Airport, JetBlue flies to Havana. From Fort Lauderdale, they fly to Havana, Santa Clara, Holguin, and Camaguey.

https://www.jetblue.com/flights/cuba/

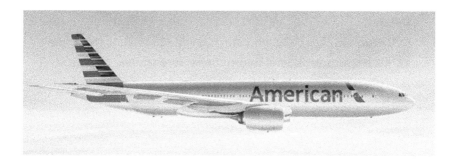

American:

American Airlines flies several daily, non-stop services to Cuba. They originate in Miami and fly to Havana, Varadero, Holguin, and Santa Clara.

https://www.aa.com/i18n/plan-travel/destinations/cuba.jsp?anchorLocation=DirectURL&title=cuba

Southwest:

Southwest Airlines flies from Tampa and Fort Lauderdale, to Havana and Santa Clara.

https://www.southwest.com/html/promotions/new-service-cuba.html

Alaska:

Alaska Airlines flies from Los Angeles to Havana, which is excellent, as it's the one and only airline that flies from the West Coast. LAX is obviously a big hub so anyone in Seattle, Portland, San Francisco, or San Diego can connect here.

https://www.alaskaair.com/content/cities/flights-to/cuba.aspx

Frontier:
Frontier has daily, direct services from Miami to Havana.

https://www.flyfrontier.com/travel-information/international-travel-and-security/cuba/

Most airlines have a separate check-in desk for Cuba flights and additional screening plus a desk for the tourist card, if you didn't purchase it in advance. If you are connecting to Cuba, an agent will be present at the gate to sell tourist cards - you don't need to buy it at your originating airport.

All of the above links to the airlines take you to a detailed page where each airline outlines their own regulations and instructions for traveling to Cuba. Much of that information is detailed in this book but for individual airlines, please refer to the links.

Baggage restrictions are in place for Cuba with certain airlines. Some do not permit more than two checked bags and you may be subject to more scrutiny. As always, standard TSA regulations apply to traveling out of the United States, for example the 3-1-1 liquids rule. This will also apply if you transit from Cuba out to another Caribbean destination before returning to the US.

Chapter Seven: Tour Group Packages

For travelers that are interested in seeing quite a lot of Cuba in a short period of time, a tour group may be the way to go. There are tours tailored to almost every kind of travel. Often, the tours run under the people to people license and have set itineraries with meaningful interactions with Cubans that satisfy the American government requirements for legal travel.

Other benefits of an organized tour is that you don't have to plan your own trip and research what sort of schedule you need to set for yourself. You don't need to book any hotels or guesthouses, and you will be able to travel with less cash on your person since the tour company will cover all the major expenses.

What do tours of Cuba entail? How do you know what the best tour for you is? And how do you know that you're choosing a tour that will be legal for Americans? We cover that, and a bit more in this chapter.

What do tours of Cuba entail?

Of the tours researched from a variety of tour operators, the tours range from six day/seven night tours to 21 night tours. Obviously the longer the trip, the more you do, but some of the longer trips are not designated with Americans in mind and don't fulfill the requirements necessary for the general licenses. For example, there are several tour operators that run sailing trips around Cuba. As much fun as that sounds, spending a week onboard a luxury yacht is most definitely illegal in the eyes of the American government. Neither is a week-long cycling trip legal.

That being said, there are some incredible tours out there that cater to American travelers while still providing non-cookie cutter experiences. You will need to research the different tours to find one that suits your needs.

It is worth noting, before going into detail, that itineraries for tours in Cuba are tentative. All the websites list an itinerary, but they also add the much-needed caveat that things in Cuba don't always go to plan.

Tours of Cuba for American citizens generally entail a welcome meeting at your hotel in Havana, then getting on the road the next day. At this meeting, you will get the final itinerary and any additional information.

All tours for Americans run under the people to people license so your itinerary will be a mixture of meeting locals and visiting attractions while the head of a department gives you a tour or a lecture. Depending on the tour you have booked, you may be visiting a local school and interacting with the teachers and students or visiting a coffee plantation and walking the fields with a worker, learning firsthand the way that coffee is harvested.

All tours include a night of accommodation before the tour begins and all accommodation during the tour. Some of this accommodation may be in hotels, and some of it may be in *casa particulares*. Your itinerary should state where you'll be staying.

Keep in mind that it may not meet your American standards of hotels but that it's still all part of the adventure. Many do not allow you to stay longer than the tour because you will not have the organization's help to facilitate legal interactions with Cubans. Some tours include a domestic flight between Havana and another city; others mandate that you must make those domestic flight arrangements yourself by contacting their reservations desk. You will need to purchase the domestic flights separately from the tour itself.

International flights are also not included in the tour costs. Several tour operators give you a recommended flight, where they provide complimentary airport to hotel transfer if you book that flight. Others do not. If self-transfer between the airport and the hotel is something you and your travel companions do not wish to undertake, consider a tour that covers that for you.

Each and every tour is different depending on the operator you go with. Some tours are very small, no more than twelve travelers. Others are larger, around 20-25. The larger tours often stay in larger hotels, whereas small, independent tours prefer to stay in bed and breakfasts, known as *casa particulares* in Cuba. These are small, family run homestays that benefit the family and local community, not the Cuban government.

These are several tour operators we have researched:

Insight Cuba
https://insightcuba.com/cuba-travel

Conocer Cuba Travel *★Recommended*
http://www.conocercubatravel.com/

Cuban Adventures USA
http://www.cubanadventuresusa.com

In our opinion, these are among the best. Intrepid is another tour operator you may come across, and while they have some amazing tours, only one is legal for US citizens. You are not permitted to book the cycling tour or the Grand Cuba tour - there is only one option with Intrepid and that is the Hola Cuba Tour for Americans.

What does a tour cost?

Insight Cuba
For a 6 nights, 7 days Cuba tour, you can expect to pay around $5500. Shorter trips are less; with Insight Cuba, a weekend (4 nights, 3 days) tour is $3400. Trips that include more will run a little on the higher end.

Conocer Cuba
A 7-day, 6-night itinerary featuring multiple cities is about $1265. Conocer Cuba has various local connections on the island that make for an authentic travel experience, and is among the most economical options for exploring the real Cuba.

Cuban Adventures USA
The 9 day tour starts at $1600. Solo travelers can pay a single supplement of $440 to ensure they have their own room.

What do I need to know once I've booked my tour?

Once you've booked your tour, here's a bit more information. Check with the tour operator about flights. In general, it is good practice to book the recommended flight as you'll get the shuttle service and get a chance to meet some of your fellow travelers before the tour begins.

Remember that you will need to also have medical insurance but that it will be included in the airline price. Keep your boarding pass with you at all times to prove you have the insurance policy.

Because the tour guides will handle the majority of the monetary transactions, you don't need to worry about traveling with a lot of money. Not all meals are covered either, so you will be shelling out a bit of cash for a few meals, drinks, and gratuities. It is also smart to have enough cash to cover the occasional taxi, any souvenirs, or other incidentals.

Remember that you cannot exchange American dollars without incurring a 10% penalty so if the price is right, it's best to exchange your US dollars for Euros before leaving the US and then changing the Euros for CUC once you are in Cuba. Also remember that ATMs are very scarce and even if you do find one, they will have high fees and don't accept American credit or debit cards.

Most tour operators suggest between US $300 - $500 per person for incidentals.

After booking your tour, you need to ...

... purchase the Cuban tourist card if not already included in your airline ticket. Remember to check with your airline about where to buy it. It is possible to buy it online, but you will need to know the processing time and not leave it too late.

... exchange your US dollars for foreign currency like Euros or British Pound Sterling. You will convert them to Cuban currency on arrival in Cuba.

... purchase travel insurance. Your medical insurance is included in your airline ticket, but if anything happens to your flights or to your tour, travel insurance will cover that. It may also cover you if you need to cancel the trip last minute due to a family emergency or other issue. Read the fine print before purchasing, of course. World Nomads is a very good travel insurance operator.

… understand that traveling in Cuba is an adventure. Things do not always go to plan. Power cuts are common, hot water may be a luxury, and some toilets don't have seats. Regardless, your trip to Cuba will be one of the most rewarding trips of your lifetime.

In the next chapter, we'll take a closer look at the cities in Cuba and what you should visit while you are there!

Chapter Eight: Cities of Cuba

In this chapter, we'll explore the cities to visit in different regions of the island.

Havana

Havana is, by several million, the largest city in Cuba, and most likely the city that you will fly into when heading to Cuba. Several other cities do cater to international flights from Miami, Fort Lauderdale, and Tampa (see the above chapter on airlines), like Santa Clara, Holguin, and Camaguey, but your tour will either begin or end in Havana. If you aren't taking a group tour, Havana should still be on your list; you would be doing your travels a great injustice if you don't spend a few days in Havana!

Far from being a remote outpost of Caribbean culture, Havana is a bustling, energetic city with a vibrancy that exceeds expectations and exudes flair. It has the majority of the national museums, a nightlife that reminds one of Miami, and iconic streets filled with statues of former revolutionaries, old pastel colored cars, and throngs of locals.

In any other city, the rundown buildings that line Havana's streets, the bright laundry that hangs overhead, the potholed streets, these would be frowned upon; here they are celebrated as part of the city's impressive culture. There are tons of historical walks in Havana that take you past once-important plazas, statues, and consular buildings. The 16th and 17th century castellos would be what protected the city, and the view from many of them is spectacular. Havana's malecon, the seaside promenade, is one of the city's most popular meeting places. During the day it's filled with fishermen and by night, friends and lovers.

Havana's best attractions include the Castillo el Morro, packed with art and displaying vivid architecture, the Cathedral Havana, which lies in the same square that houses four of Cuba's richest families, the Necropolis Cristobal Colon, and the Almacenes San Jose market.

Cuba's sports culture is also highly evident in Havana. Wandering down any street, you'll very likely happen upon a pickup basketball, football, or baseball game. If you feel up for it, join in for a minute. Havana is also where all the professional teams play. Go to a match if you can; tickets are very cheap and it's relatively easy to get in. You won't be able to buy a ticket in advance, so head for the stadium early to ensure you get a seat. Watching Cuban baseball is by far one of the highlights in professional sports. These guys are passionate about the sport in a way that US players have lost, and the crowd is wild about the game.

Baracoa

Remote and hard to access, Cuba's first settlement Baracoa is still one of Cuba's prettiest cities. Tucked away in between the Atlantic Ocean and the rainforest-covered mountains, it still retains its pristine colonial image; it was actually cut off from the rest of Cuba for nearly 500 years, until Fidel Castro had the winding mountain road built. A popular activity, if you have the free time, is to hike El Yunque, the mountain looming over town. Baracoa is also a foodie's dream town, with incredibly fresh seafood and fresh fruit making up a majority of the town's menus alongside the local chocolate and cucurucho (pineapple-coconut-palm leaf candies) factories. It's a very tropical town, and it rains a lot, but its isolation means that it's a very original and unique town to explore.

Camaguey

Described by several writers as a labyrinth, and supposedly built this way to confuse pirates and marauders, Camaguey is an energetic, artistic city that doesn't have the same lure for travelers, but it's still worth a visit. If your travels fall under the support for Cuban people, people to people, or education licenses, visiting Camaguey is perfect, as you'll get the chance to meet local artists and speak with them about their influences, their work, and their lives. Camaguey is another UNESCO World Heritage-listed site, should the history and arts appeal to you.

Cienfuegos

More French than Spanish, Cienfuegos was once the region's busiest trading port. It was founded in the early 19th century by French traders and the architecture is more modern than some other Cuban cities. Cienfuegos is a great jumping off point to visit the Bay of Pigs (two hours away) or the popular pools at Rio Hanabanilla' waterfalls. There's plenty of art here, from various galleries to museums, and the town also pays homage to Jose Marti, the Cuban exile who staged the late 19th century revolution, pre-Guevara and Castro brothers.

Your first impression of Cinefuegos may be that it feels very western, very European. Your instincts would be right; even Cubans say that Cienfuegos has a different feel to it, not for the worse. Known as the Pearl of the South, or the Paris of Cuba, Cienfuegos also has a number of good snorkeling and scuba diving spots among its many reefs.

Santa Clara

Anyone with a passing interest in Cuban history - and let's face it, how could you not be intrigued by the country? - shouldn't miss Santa Clara, home to the revolutionary who toppled the Batista regime, Che Guevara. The Argentinian-born guerrilla soldier adopted Santa Clara as home (his wife was from here) and base before aligning with the Castro brothers to wage war against the government. Plenty of monuments pay homage to El Che, from national museums to small statues you may stumble upon. The mausoleum which holds his remains is one of the most popular attractions here, as is the Tren Blindado Park where the battle of Santa Clara is depicted.

For a great view of the city, climb the Loma del Capiro. This mountain offers a stunning panorama of the city and was also a strategic point in Guevara's war.

Santiago de Cuba

Santiago de Cuba may be the best place in Cuba to enjoy the music. Cuba's second city is home to the popular Casa de la Trova, which is both a local and a tourist hotspot. The vibe here is very musical and it's easy to fall into the relaxed way of life here. As a city that's geographically closer to Haiti and the Dominican Republic than to Havana, the influences here lean more toward Afro-Caribbean rather than Cuban. Santiago hosts one of the best Carnaval festivals in Cuba.

Santiago is also home to several important historical homes. As Cuba's first capital, Santiago has a rich history unparalleled by Havana or Trinidad. Highlights of Santiago include the Castillo de San Pedro de la Roca, Parque Cespedes, and Casa de Diego Velázquez, the oldest residence in Cuba and former home of the conquistador and colonial governor. Don't miss the popular Tivoli neighborhood, the old French quarter settled by Haitian colonists in the 18th century, where you can also climb the picturesque Padre Pico steps.

Nearby attractions are the town of El Cobre, where a much-venerated statue of the Virgin de la Caridad lives at the basilica.

Religious enthusiasts will enjoy the culture and the history behind El Cobre.

Trinidad

Trinidad is famously known as the city stuck in time, and it's evident when you arrive that things won't be the same. The colonial architecture, the cobblestone streets, and the horse-drawn carts hark back to a simpler time, but it can be a frustrating city to spend an excessive amount of time in. Power cuts are common, internet is nonexistent, and food may not be quite what you're used to. Still, to see a side of Old Cuba, UNESCO World Heritage-listed Trinidad is where to go. With the Escambray Mountains behind it and the long white sand beaches on the edge, it consistently ranks as one of travelers favorite cities in Cuba.

Varadero

Cuba's leisurely beach region, with picturesque white sand beaches stretching for miles along the turquoise colored sea, Varadero is home to the all-inclusive resorts. For this reason, I recommend skipping this region since it doesn't give you much of a real Cuban experience.

You will not get a feel for Cuba here, as a gate at the entrance to the city keeps out the Cubans, but if you want a luxury resort with as many trimmings as Cuba can give you, it's where to go.

Unfortunately, spending time in Varadero is illegal under the US government regulations, and as not-Cuba as Varadero is, your time is better spent elsewhere.

Vinales

More a regional capital than a true city, Vinales nonetheless is a great place to visit to get a glimpse into rural Cuban life. It is home to the many tobacco fields - all the big names get their tobacco leaves here, regardless of where the factory is. Much more laid back and sleepier than any of the other towns in Cuba, Vinales is a picture-perfect village. It's located in the Pinar del Rios region, home to more tobacco fields and sugarcane plantations.

Chapter Nine: What To Do in Cuba Once You Are There

Cuban Museums

Many of the national museums are in Havana. As part of your itinerary, you'll likely be visiting a fair few of them and meeting the directors. Some of the more important ones are the Museo de la Revolución, where you will get a better understanding of Cuban culture and history, and the Felipe Poey Natural History Museum, which houses a "significant chunk of scientific samples," many the only of their kind in Cuba.

Havana is also home to the national art museums; there is the museum of fine arts, decorative arts, ceramic arts, colonial art, and religious art. In nearby San Francisco de Paula is the former home of Ernest Hemingway, writer and expat. It was home to the Hemingway family for 20+ years, and after his death went to the Cuban government. Literature lovers shouldn't miss this one; it's a short drive from Havana city.

In Trinidad, a living museum on its own, don't miss the Architectural Museum, which showcases the many different architectural styles of the 18th and 19th centuries. Another good museum in Trinidad is Romantic Museum, housed in an 19th century mansion called Brunet Palace, and home to a variety of 18th and 19th century arts and furniture (the Romantic era). In addition to the many displays of jewels, arts, ceramics, and more that lined the houses of Cuban aristocracy. There is also a recreated 19th century bathroom. Another excellent museum in Trinidad is the Archaeological Museum, which highlights the pre-Colombian civilizations in Cuba.

Baracoa's main museum is the Museo Municipal, which highlights the Taino people, who lived here long before any colonists arrived.

Santa Clara's main attraction is the Che Guevara Mausoleum, which in addition to being where his remains are (having been returned to Cuba in the 1990s after his well-publicized Bolivian execution in 1967), is a well-appointed museum about his life. Among the many documents are details explaining how this Argentinian-born rebel became the face of the Cuban Revolution.

Che Guevara

Cuban Nightlife

We would be remiss to not talk about the Cuban nightlife! Any journalist, blogger, or photographer - really, anyone - who has gone to Cuba has returned with stories and images that paint a wildly exciting, powerfully rich, Afro-Caribbean influenced night scene. From the salsa dancers to the lush colors and the lights, from the pop sounds mixed with the strum of a tropical instrument, from the thumping DJ booths to the beat of a drum, Cuban nightlife is the highlight of many a traveler.

Havana is of course the center of the nightlife, where you'll find a majority of new clubs, bars, and cafes that cater to a late night crowd, but don't underestimate the smaller towns. Even remote

Baracoa has a wildly entertaining street scene where you'll find people of all ages dancing well into the night to the sounds of a local band.

In Trinidad, hit the streets to see the music. Almost every plaza and street corner will have a band, so lively is the city. You'll also find an underground scene in Trinidad, unlike anything else found in Cuba. A very popular nightlife spot in Trinidad is in a cave, which attracts locals of all kinds who come to dance the night away.

Expect to pay a cover charge for most bars and clubs; some include a drink as part of the cover but don't be surprised if it doesn't. You'll still be getting a good deal.

Outside of the Cities

Getting out of the cities to explore Cuba's beaches, tobacco fields, and national parks should definitely be on your itinerary. If you are part of a tour, your itinerary likely includes a visit to at least one of these, where you will meet the field hands, wine experts, and rangers at the park. Solo, this may be more difficult to fit into your expected itinerary, but you should make the effort, as several of the parks are UNESCO World Heritage Sites for their impressive landscapes.

Pinar del Rio

The furthest west of the Cuban regions, Pinar del Rio is Cuba's mountainous agricultural area. Known mainly for its tobacco fields and coffee plantations, the Vinales Valley is a UNESCO World Heritage site because of its *mogotes* - limestone outcroppings - and traditional architecture. Pinar is well worth the drive from Havana, and some tours do get you there.

Three of the most popular activities in the Vinales Valley is caving, hiking, and rock climbing. New routes through the limestone caves are constantly being discovered, so the area is becoming more and more tourism-based.

Cuban Beaches

Cuba has some legendary beaches, from the expanses of white sand at Varadero to the remote beaches that you find at the end of a dirt road. As an American traveler, you can't spend the majority of your time on the beach but you are allowed some free time. Hitting a beach, soaking up the Caribbean sun, and sipping a Cuba Libre is one way to do it.

Some of the more popular beaches that also have some historical or cultural significance include Isla de la Juventud, where prisons held - at different times - Jose Marti and Fidel Castro and Maria la Gorda, for its unparalleled diving opportunities.

As mentioned above, Varadero - while a luxurious beach and a haven for all-inclusive seekers - isn't one of the best ways to really understand Cuba. It does, however, have one of Cuba's longest beaches and is rarely crowded.

National Parks in Cuba

While it doesn't have as many national parks as the US or Canada, for a small country, Cuba certainly has its fair share of them.

Many are UNESCO sites, due in part to the lack of tourism and man-made infrastructure that permeates western countries.

Vinales Valley, in the Pinar del Rio region (above) is a national park of extreme importance. The karstic formations are among some of the best in the world and are still mostly undiscovered by non-serious trampers.

Nearby is the **Reserva de la Biosfera Sierra del Rosario**, not a national park but a UNESCO-protected biosphere reserve in the Sierra del Rosario mountains. The tourism here is centered around two main towns, Soroa and Las Terrazas.

Both are much smaller than Vinales, but Soroa is by far the smaller of the two. There are some excellent things to see in the reserve, most impressively the world's second largest orchid garden at the Orquideario Soroa. Take a short hike up the hills behind the garden to a ruined mansion and panoramic views of the mountains. For a longer hike, head to the ruined Cafetal Independencia coffee plantation, which is six hours from Soroa.

On the peninsula south of Havana and west of Cienfuegos, **Parque Nacional Cienaga de Zapata** is considered one of the best birdwatching national parks in the world. It is similar to the Everglades National Park in scope and in wildlife. There is a crocodile park there, where they breed crocs, and the birdlife is outstanding. The Bay of Pigs is just to the east. This region where Fidel Castro defeated the US/exile guerillas is full of history and a great place to understand just why the poor regions of Cuba fully stand behind the Communist government. More a collection of parks than one park, the Gran Parque Natural Topes de Collantes is a network of mountains, caves, waterfalls, and history that spans three regions: Cienfuegos, Villa Clara, and Santi Spiritus.

Some of the parklands still fall under military jurisdiction and are inaccessible to the public but much is open for hiking, caving, fishing, and more. The parks lie in the Escambray Mountains, which hid both anti-Batista rebels during the revolution and anti-Castro rebels afterwards. There are several developed tourist regions in the park. They include: Parque Altiplano, Parque Codina, Parque Guanayara, Parque El Nicho, Parque El Cubano, and Embalse Hanabanilla.

For some trails you are required to have a guide; if you're traveling as part of a tour group then you this will be taken care of, but if you are solo then don't expect to show up and hike - you will need to hire a guide in advance.

Chapter Ten: Spanish Schools in Cuba

Many people head to Central America and the Caribbean to immerse themselves in a Spanish school. While each country has a slightly different dialect, learning Spanish from a local perspective certainly has its benefits, not the least of which is the almost complete immersion into both the language and the Cuban culture.

Why learn Spanish in Cuba?

As an American, learning Spanish in Cuba means that you can head there under the **educational license**, which allows for a bit more free time than some of the others, since you're expected to maintain a full-time school schedule.

By enrolling in a Spanish language course in Cuba you may stay with a local family, share meals with them, and learn Spanish from locals as well as your instructor. Or you'll be placed in an apartment for the duration of your stay, giving you time to explore the city on your own or with your new classmates. Cubans have a zest for life found in few other places, and you'll soak it up while you wander the city as part of your course.

Most Spanish schools in Cuba are also relatively new, so you'll be studying with instructors who have worked in other Spanish schools in other places. They have access to audio/visual equipment, air-conditioned classrooms, and internet. Classes are small, which means ample one on one time with the instructors. Below is a small list of schools we've researched with a little bit about each one.

Sprachcaffe Language School
Havana

Sprachcaffe is one of the leading language schools in the world, having courses in over seven languages in more than twelve countries. Their Havana-based courses are very popular. The classroom is located in the Miramar district, which is the upscale, fashionable neighborhood in Havana. The courses are only offered to adults, meaning that your new classmates and you can meet at Havana's dance clubs or bars after hours to indulge in some of the culture.

For more information, go to http://www.sprachcaffe.com/english/adults-spanish-courses-cuba/havana.htm

Cactus Language School
Havana

Cactus, a UK-based language school, has been doing it for a long time. Their courses, based in Havana, are small and accredited, so if you're thinking of taking a language course for university, you could possibly get credit with this one. Definitely confirm this before booking. They also offer pre-trip courses to give you a head start, plus one on one instructions and email access to your instructor.

For more information, go to http://www.cactuslanguage.com/adults/locations/spanish/cuba/

Jakera Language School
Havana

Jakera consistently ranks as one of the top language schools in Havana. This is a popular choice for younger travelers; the average age of students with Jakera is 28 and the accommodation provided is typically in hostels. Jakera runs very small classes - the average class size is only six students! They give students the afternoons free to enjoy the city and also offer courses or activities for students to participate in.

For more information, go to
http://www.languagecourse.net/school-jakera-havana.php3

Enforex
Havana, Santiago de Cuba, Trinidad

While this program has their main campus in Havana, they also offer Spanish courses in Santiago and Trinidad. If you are keen to learn Spanish from a local but don't want to live in Havana, Enforex might be a better option because you can live in a different city and see a different side to Cuban life. Courses are small and intimate, often held in a host family's house or at the instructor's home.

For more information, go to…
- Havana location: http://www.enforex.com/course-havana.html
- Santiago location: http://www.enforex.com/latinamerica-cuba-santiago.html
- Trinidad location: http://www.enforex.com/latinamerica-cuba-trinidad.html

Conclusion

Now that the restrictions on travel in Cuba have eased, it's easier to travel there as an American. It is not free rein travel, but as long as you comply with the US government regulations, you shouldn't have any problems in traveling to and from Cuba.

In the first few chapters, we covered a brief history of Cuba and why the trade embargo and travel restrictions were in place to begin with, and the practical things needed for a trip to Cuba - like what language they speak, what the currency is, and other details about traveling to Cuba.

In chapters four and five, we looked at the governmental regulations including the thirteen license that you can apply under, and how to get a tourist card for Cuba. Chapter six discussed the American airlines that fly to Cuba and what routes there are. Chapter seven talked about tour packages and why that might be a better option if you're traveling solo or not in a position to plan your own trip.

The remainder of this book looked at what to do in Cuba once you're there, from the different cities and what to see in each one to the national parks and the famous beaches.

Cuba is a wonderful country with incredibly warm and welcoming people. We are sure that once you go, you'll want to return.

From the stunning endless beaches to the rugged rainforest-covered mountains, the pervasive salsa music to the chaotic stadiums, Cuba has it all.

Lightning Source UK Ltd.
Milton Keynes UK
UKHW051106280220
359457UK00026B/308